Love remains

Jeffrey Elliott-Cruz

LOVE REMAINS
Copyright © 2021 by Jeffrey Elliott-Cruz

All rights reserved. No part of this publication may be reproduced, distributed, or transmitted in any form or by any means, including photocopying, recording, or other electronic or mechanical methods, without the prior written permission of the publisher or author, except in the case of brief quotations embodied in critical reviews and certain other noncommercial uses permitted by copyright law.

Although every precaution has been taken to verify the accuracy of the information contained herein, the author and publisher assume no responsibility for any errors or omissions. No liability is assumed for damages that may result from the use of information contained within.

Library of Congress Control Number: 2021914943
ISBN-13:   Paperback: 978-1-64749-571-8
           ePub: 978-1-64749-572-5

Printed in the United States of America

GoTo Publish
GoToPublish LLC
1-888-337-1724
www.gotopublish.com
info@gotopublish.com

Contents

The Swan Of My Heart 2
Yesteryears Journey 4
The Compass 6
The Mortality Of Mankind 8
Spirit Of Christ 10
Like A Stream 12
A Time Of Beauty 14
Rhyme Time 2 16
My Vow To Pledge, ...18
Love Without End 18
Eternity In Your Eyes 20
My Vow (Sonnet 2) 22
My Beautiful Queen Of My Heart (Sonnet 2) 24
Trust God 26
My Heart Whispers Love 28
My Beautiful Moonbeam 30
My Life Overflows 32
Only You 34
Reflection Of Destiny 36
Tender Moments 38
Allure Of Love 40
Chimes And bells Of Love 42
God's Love 44
Lover's Blessing 46
Speak Of You 48
We Shall Forever Embrace 50
In The Morning 52

Temple To The Goddess Of Love	54
Within The Chambers Of The Heart	56
Just One Tender And Sweet Kiss	58
My Love Remains True	60
Love Infuses Heart And Soul	62
Is The Greatest Of All God's Gifts	64
Love's Circle - Epilogue	66
The Beauty	68
My Heart Belongs To You	70
A Time Of Love	72
A Pledge	72
My Love Overflows	74
Love Is Always	76
Minutes	78
The Depth Of Love	80
Close To You	82
Eterity In Your Eyes	84
Love In Essence	84
My Peach	86
My Lover's Gentle Touch	86
Adilene's Faith	88
My Heart Can Never Let You Go	90
Love Means Forgiveness	90
True Lover's Serenade	92
Love Is A Time Of Innocence	92
In God's Light	94
Her Love Is My Declaration	95
Healing Rose Of Sharon	96
Passions Of Desire	97
Silent Moments	98

Photo credits to Adilene Idalie/ Betty Sharon

Thank you!

The Swan Of My Heart

BY JEFFREY ELLIOTT-CRUZ

My lover is as graceful
As a beautiful swan
Shimmering and gliding
Upon the water
In fashionable poise
And surreal loveliness
 and beauty
As she glides across
The waters of life
Her life's ripples of grace
And stunning appropriation
Flow with her charm
To my heart
And capture my heart
Embraced by her gorgeous beauty
She transforms her essence
Into the swan of my heart
So that my love remains

Yesteryears Journey

BY JEFFREY ELLIOTT-CRUZ

Whereupon mighty pharaohs
reigned over Egypt's fame
Alexander prince fought
for power and gain
Athens, Sparta, Egypt fade
Life tis a dream
Life's journey is only a fortnight
In time the vestal virgins
beauty fades
The vestal's temple declines
and decays
In the blink of an historic eye
In turn each claim to fame
Now only old ruins
and history books remain
Like the mighty pharaohs
Dust in the sand
But my mistress
Love's remains
As life still sustains
Life's journey is a fortnight

The Compass

BY JEFFREY ELLIOTT-CRUZ

God's grace speaks softly to my heart
As a whisper in the gentle wind
As morning dew impressed
and imprinted upon my mind
As the most beautiful music
Which plays to my soul
Uplifts my spirit
Enlivens my mind
Like a morning dew
Impressed heart and mind
As guiding light
To find my love
Upon my faith
In our eternal vows
From out of the wilderness
Points the way home
To my lover's arms
Finding God's firm directions
Speaks peace to my
Heart and mind
Faith and Gods impressions
To my love and home
Like a compass

The Mortality Of Mankind

BY JEFFREY ELLIOTT-CRUZ

Before this world
Was created and mortality
Before the recordation
Of the days of man
In that time Gods
Organized matter
And created the worlds
and stars
Filled the vast
darkness of space
With the light of worlds,
My lover and I,
Joined together, merged
In an eternal bound
Our spirits intermingled

Spirit Of Christ

BY JEFFREY ELLIOTT-CRUZ

The spirit of Christ
Shall be found
In the whisper
Of the breeze
The rustling of leaves
The gentle warmth
Of the morning sun
The fresh dew
Upon the flowers
And nature's lawn
Which also imprints
Upon you're heart
and mind
The small voice
Which in the still
Of the morning
Speaks to your soul
So your mind and heart
Is impressed
These things disclose
Our Lover's souls
Eternally covenanted
In a sacred union
Forever as one
The spirit of Christ

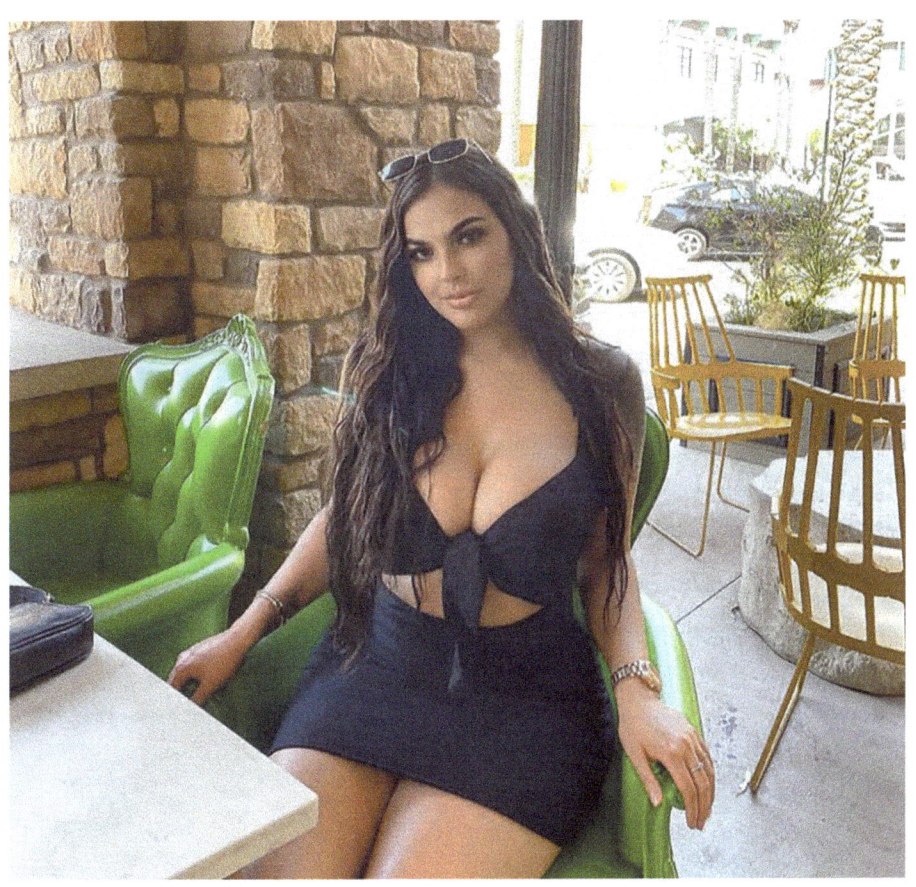

Like A Stream

BY JEFFREY ELLIOTT-CRUZ

The nature of life
Is like water moving
In a stream
To the ocean teeming with life
A heavenly aspect
In God's eternal plan
Love eternally remains
Life is moving
Like a swift river
To the source of all life
As part of a grandeur design
Tis the more profound impact
Of life
To love and love again

A Time Of Beauty

BY JEFFREY ELLIOTT-CRUZ

In the time of beauty
My love blossomed
As a wonderful flower
In the garden of God's creation
Radiant, magnificent , wonderfully lovely
The gorgeous rose of Sharon
The most pleasing and lovely Rose
 in the garden of earthly wonders and delights
As radiant and lovely as her appearance
God's gift to her
Is the beauty she holds in her heart and soul
The beautiful mistress of God's garden
Forever unspoiled by the transient corruptions
But a pure delight of Heavenly design
A heavenly gift
The wonderful rose of Sharon

Rhyme Time 2

BY JEFFREY ELLIOTT-CRUZ

What's your prime
Mine is nine
Stay in time
Always be mine
All the time
That's so fine
Beat in time
That's the nine
What's so fine
Homeboys rhyme
Have'n a good time
Hood prime time
What's your prime
Mine is nine

My Vow To Pledge, Love Without End

BY JEFFREY ELLIOTT-CRUZ

In you, my love has been fulfilled
I can make love to no other
My dreams of my lover
Have all been satisfied
There can never be another
I will never kiss another women's lips
Nor seek refuge in another's arms
Heaven has sent you
To me as a gift
You are my complete satisfaction
No other woman can quench my thirst
Nor satiate my hunger
A simple look from you
Fills my heart with wonder
My vow to pledge
To keep and hold
To love you forever and ever
A vow to pledge
A love without end
A heart to hold
A soul to keep
I vow I am yours
Forever and ever
My sweet Adilene

Eternity In Your Eyes

BY JEFFREY ELLIOTT-CRUZ

Throughout my life
And in space and time
My heart yearns for love
My life is but a bitter course
Without the recompense
Of your precious love
Without the benefit of your support
As the universe expands
Swells in my core
Tempers my heart
Touches my hearts most delicate strings
My hearts music plays a sweet sound
A rush of sweet melodic sound
Like a symphony fills my heart
With love's most delicate emotions
I see through love's prism
beauty and fondness
My hearts fondest desires
Eternity in your eyes

My Vow (Sonnet 2)

BY JEFFREY ELLIOTT-CRUZ

I cannot survive or thrive
Separated from her
She is my shining jewel
The precious treasure
of my life
My dream, my heart, my soul
My life's blood
My chosen heart
My sacred vow

My Beautiful Queen Of My Heart (Sonnet 2)

BY JEFFREY ELLIOTT-CRUZ

I am overwhelmed by sentiments of devotion
Awestruck by feelings of love
Humbled in majestic piety
Subject to my burning fealty
My knee bows
To the sovereign of my heart
My Queen
Enchanted by her beauty
Captivated by her charm
Mesmerized by her wonderful eyes
My knee bows
To the sovereign of my heart
My Queen
In her , I have found eternal happiness
Her happiness is also my happiness
Her success my success
Her burdens are my burdens
Her peace is my peace
My knee bows
To the sovereign of my heart
My graceful queen, my benevolent lover
The majesty of my Queen

Trust God

BY JEFFREY ELLIOTT-CRUZ

Trust God, he will lead you to the light
He surely brings salvation to you his way
Faith and hope in his divine providence
His presence to remain
His power will uphold you in his might
Trust God, he will save you from your mistakes
In salvation's grace he won't hesitate
His miracles are powerful and strong
Like Moses , he leads the way
Trust God, his prophets speak,
He surely knows the way
Trust God, his salvations saved
His lamp lights the pathway
Trust God

My Heart Whispers Love

BY JEFFREY ELLIOTT-CRUZ

My heart pumps with you for joy
My love for you is as silent as a still night
Yet as strong and mighty as an evening storm
My soul is full of love for you my sweet lover
My heart whispers love
For you are the owner of my heart
The keeper of my soul
The joy in my song
The time of my love
I am dedicated to your happiness
Confident of your loyalty
Pleased by your faithfulness
Longing for your kisses
Yearning for your touch
Inspired by your thoughtfulness
Please accept my adoration and devotion
My heart whispers love

My Beautiful Moonbeam

BY JEFFREY ELLIOTT-CRUZ

In the stillness of the night
Betwixt the setting of the sun,
The bright stars and the colors of the rising sun,
My moonbeam shines her gorgeous light,
To light up the night with her beauty and enticing charm,
Which conquers my heart,
While her moonlight dances in my soul,
And caresses my life with her gentle song,
My beautiful moonbeam's light shines bright,
She lights my life by night
Guides me, like fire by day
I am happiest
When I dance
In the light of the night,
Kissing each other,
Always together,
in a happy embrace,
My beautiful moonbeam

My Life Overflows

BY JEFFREY ELLIOTT-CRUZ

My life overflows
Like the dancing of the moon
The light of the stars
The warmth of the sun
When I bask
In the warmth and music
Of my lover
She is as a sweetly perfumed
Rose
The blessed Rose of Sharon
Love and warmth
Healing and safety
My love overflows
With God's peace
God's love remains

Only You

BY JEFFREY ELLIOTT-CRUZ

Only you , my sacred lover,
There will never be another,
You are the breath of my life,
The joy of my heart,
The happiness within my soul,
Only you, my dearest lover,
There is no other,
In you, my lover,
exists perfection for my heart,
You are the woman,
Who sings the song
which calls to my life,
My sweet companion,
my soul's delight,
My home and life,
Only you, my secret lover,
You move with me
in a lovers dance,
Dancing in my heart's
inner chamber,
Sweet lover , my soul
Hears your lover's call,
my tender kiss answers,
Only you, my sweet lover,
There will be no other,
Come to me,
we will together dance,
Until morning light,
Only you,
my sacred lover,
There will never be another

Reflection Of Destiny

BY JEFFREY ELLIOTT-CRUZ

Turn, ponder, reflect,
Look into
the mirror of repose
Upon the shimmering
Circumstances of fate
The details of destiny
The councils of free will
To determine the destiny
Of fated will
Incoherent choices
Which frolic like children
Upon the reflections
of destined fate
Into the mirror
Of time and choice

Will and destiny
Choice and circumstance
Time and decision
Merge as one
Into the mirror
Of fate
Timeless corridors
The reflection of destiny

Tender Moments

BY JEFFREY ELLIOTT-CRUZ

My feelings
For you are
Sweet and tender
Deliciously enjoyable
Harmony infused
Within the light
Of trust and respect
Our time together
Are tender moments
As a Heavenly symphony
I hear delicate melodies
Together
during our
Tender moments

Allure Of Love

BY JEFFREY ELLIOTT-CRUZ

In my dream, I saw my true love,
My true companion and love,
And was happy in my joy with her,
In my vision my love only increased,
My heart belonged to her,
Sweet lover of mine,
I was enthralled
by her sweet and kind heart,
My lover's allure,
Her kindness spoke
to the core of my soul,
Her patience calmed my agitated heart,
In time,
my lover heals my wounds,
binds my travesty
And encourages my destiny ,
My lovers allure
Our appointed destiny ,
Is to be beside my love,
My hearts pledge, my lover's vow,
My prayer of dedication,
My lover's allure

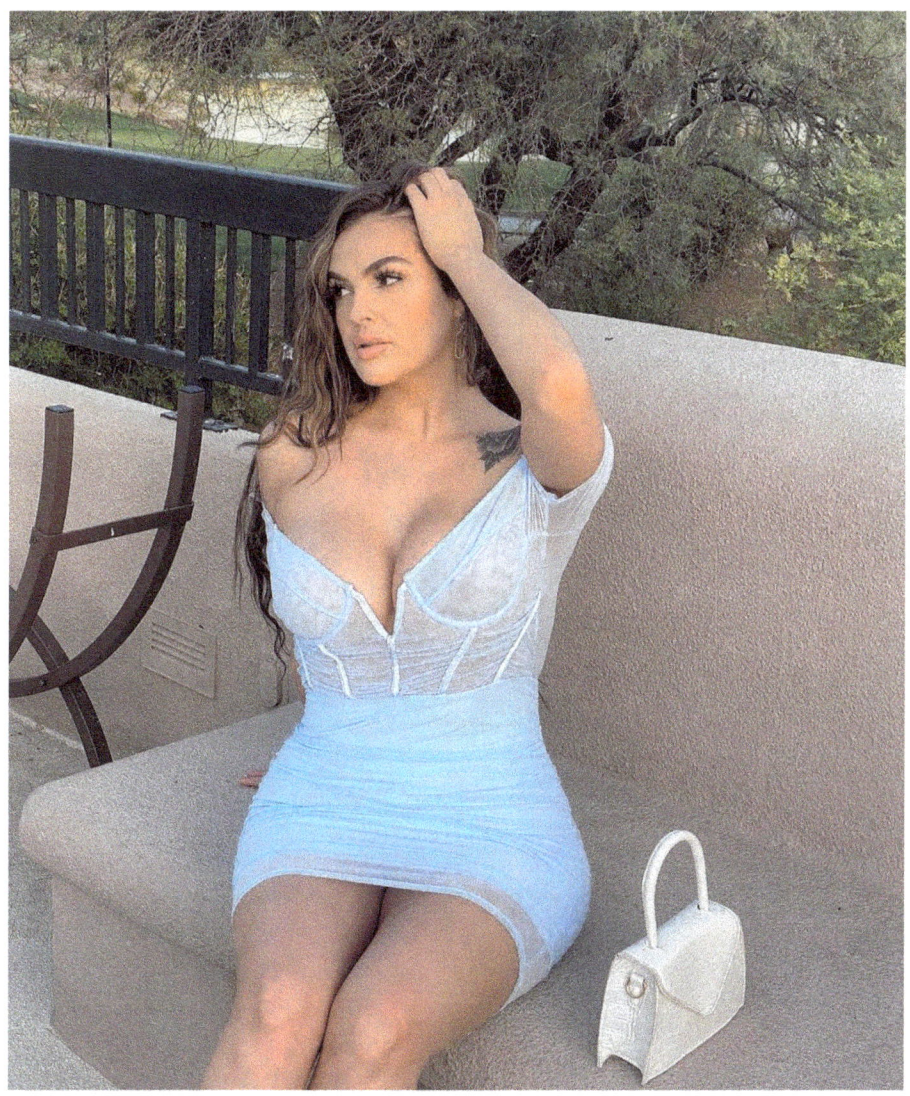

Chimes And bells Of Love

BY JEFFREY ELLIOTT-CRUZ

Sweetly sounds heavenly chimes
Chiming peace to the heart
Sweetly rings heavenly Choirs
Singing love to sooth the soul
Sweetly sounds the bells of love
Ringing love into my heart
Sweetly sounds my lover
Healing the dark and empty
Places in my heart
Sweet is the comfort
Of my mistress's kisses
Sweet is the beat
Of my lover's heart
Sweet are the chimes
And bells of love
Sweet is Adi'

God's Love

BY JEFFREY ELLIOTT-CRUZ

Tis better to enjoy
The cool drink of love
Then thirst in a drought
Of criticism, hostile hate
Tis far better
To love and enjoy
God's promise of love
Than to stew
Torment, resentment
And hate
God's love
Brings peace
Without anger or hate
Only love remains

Lover's Blessing

BY JEFFREY ELLIOTT-CRUZ

The stars whisper to the lovers
We will light your way
At night, to guide you
Along your lover's path
And the moon
Also spoke to the lovers
I will give you moonlight
By which to enjoy
Your embraces and kisses
During the dark of night
The great sun rejoiced
I will grant you
Sunshine and warmth
To warm your hearts
With love
Fire said,
I will give you fire
To warm your fireplace
And hearth
With each other's love

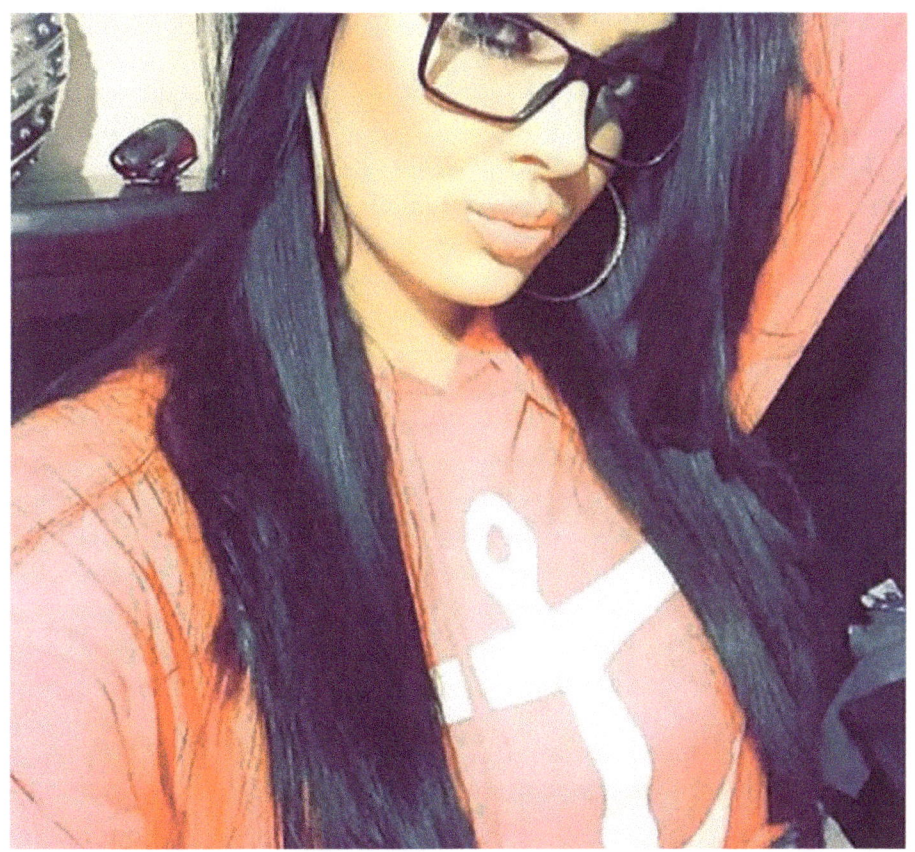

Speak Of You
BY JEFFREY ELLIOTT-CRUZ

My lips only speak of you
My dearest love
My heart only has
A lover's place for you
My sweetest love
My soul belongs to you
My sweet companion
My spirit intermingles
Spirit to spirit
With you
My faithful love
My heart is dedicated
To you
My fealty belongs
To you

LOVE REMAINS

We Shall Forever Embrace

BY JEFFREY ELLIOTT-CRUZ

Do not wait my lover
Please do not keep
Yourself from me
For I wait for your kisses
And pine for your embrace
Each night,
I am alone
My love for you
Only grows more powerful
My heart pumps more vigorously
My soul yearns for your embrace
My thirst can only be satisfied
By the sound of youre
Beating heart
By the feel of your soft skin
By the touch of your loving embrace
By the taste of your sweet lips
Like sugar and honey
Do not wait my lover
My rose of Sharon
We shall forever embrace

In The Morning

BY JEFFREY ELLIOTT-CRUZ

In the morning
With my love
And mistress
The day breaks; the sun rises
In the days young sky
A beautiful morning high
A lovely kiss from my mistress
A sweet smelling rose
Greets the day with happiness and joy
A simple sun rise ; a simple kiss
The simple things bring
The most joy
In the morning
As the sun rises
To greet a new day

Temple To The Goddess Of Love
BY JEFFREY ELLIOTT-CRUZ

In the heart full
Of empty places
And worn out spaces
Void of any traces
There is a temple
Dedicated to the
Goddess of love
If the temple gardens
Are well kept
And the goddess
Given enough respect
The temple of love
Will overflow
To fill the empty places
And worn out spaces
Like a mighty river flows
Within the sacred chambers
Of the heart
The gardens of the
Temple of love grows
As the goddess of love
A mighty river flows

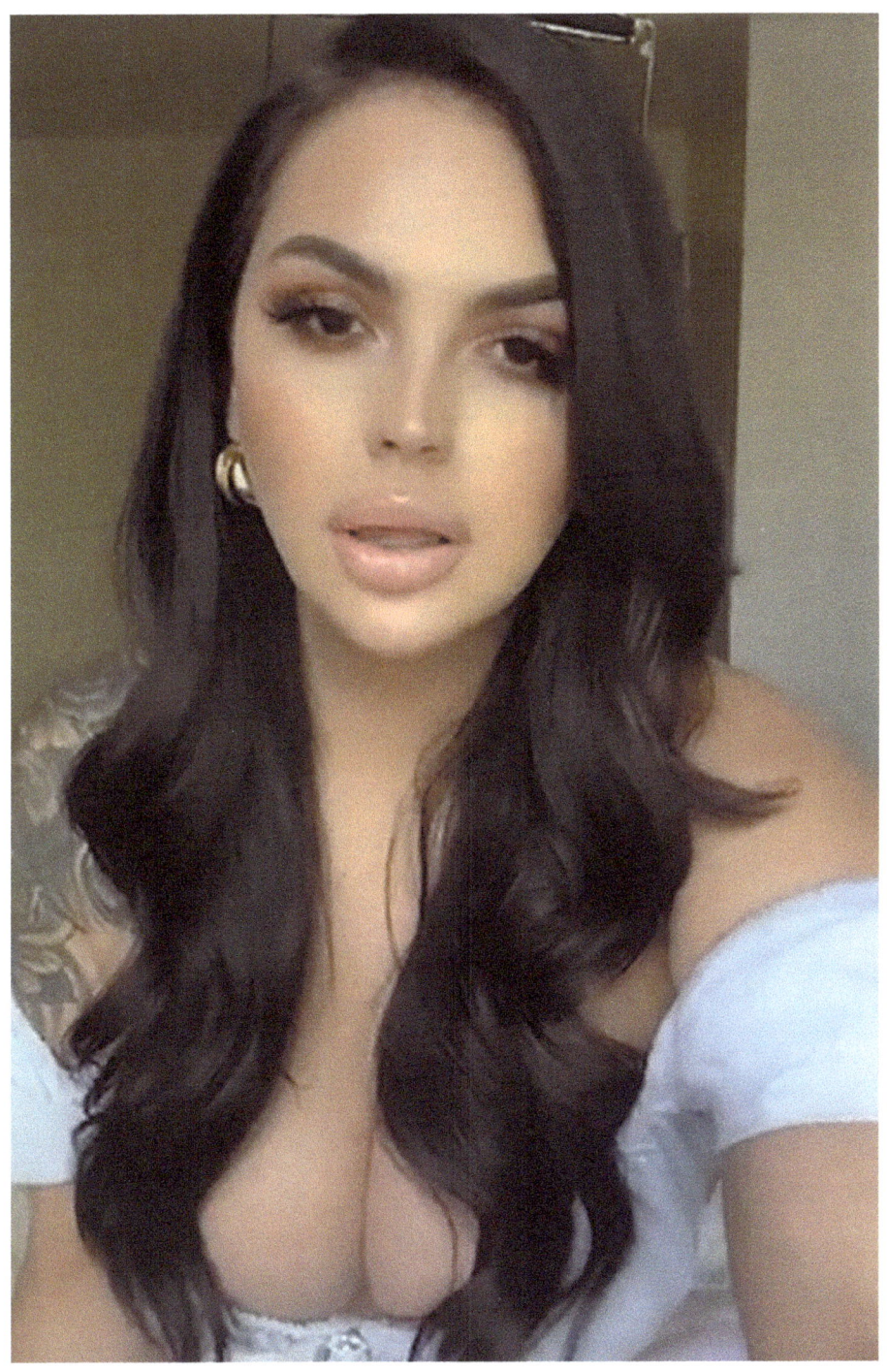

Within The Chambers Of The Heart

BY JEFFREY ELLIOTT-CRUZ

Within the deep
Recesses of the heart
In the quiet places
And also
The hearts raging passion
Love dies or grows
The sweet feelings
And fondest moments
Increase
Or as a neglected lot
Decrease to be overcome
By noxious weeds
To create despair and neglect
A cultivated garden can blossom
To adorn the sacred
Chambers of the heart
With the sweet
And colorful tapestry
Of love and life
Like the colorful flowered garden
Within the chambers
Of the heart

Just One Tender And Sweet Kiss

BY JEFFREY ELLIOTT-CRUZ

My love for you
Is gentle
Like the wind
Soft and tender
My dearest love
As soft as a gentle breeze
As sweet as a gentle kiss
As high as bright stars
Shining in the moonlight
Where I to ask for a tender kiss
To fill my heart
With your love
And my soul
With your joy and happiness
Just one sweet and tender
Kiss

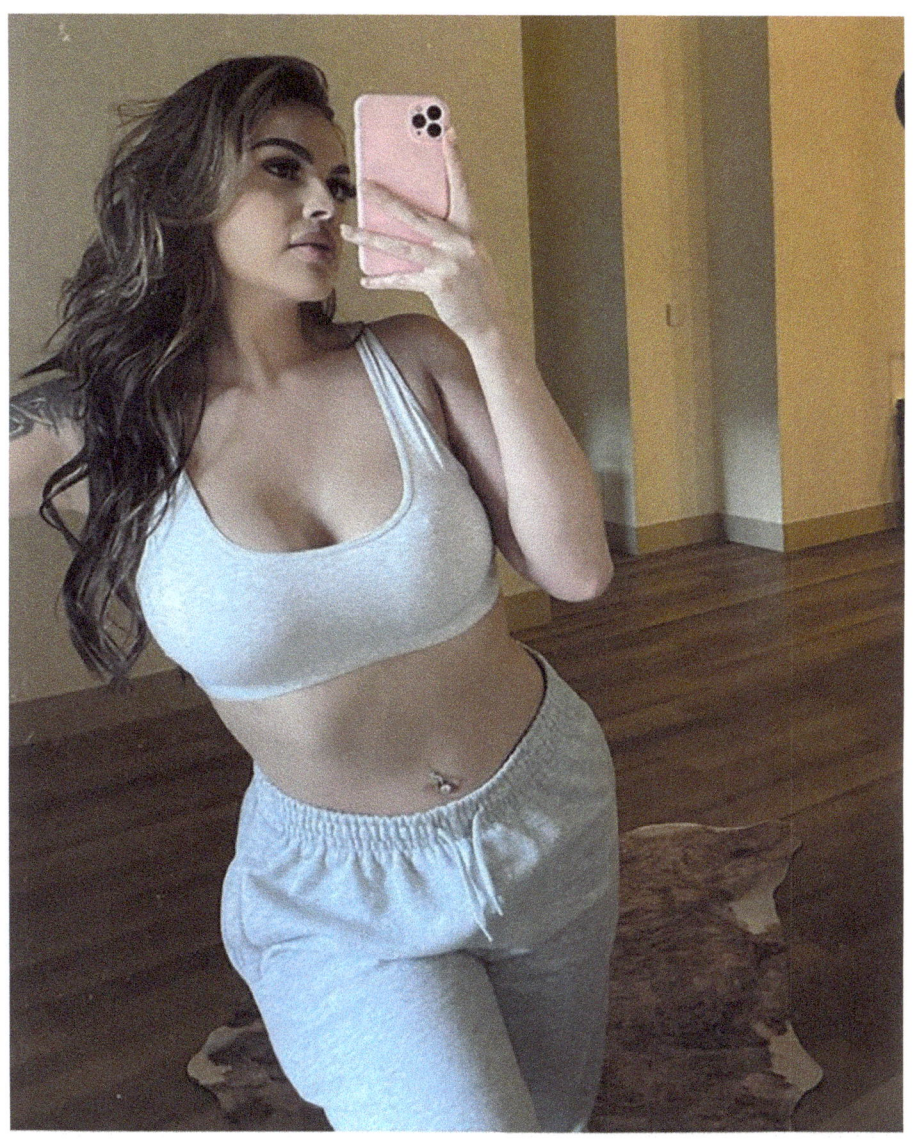

My Love Remains True

BY JEFFREY ELLIOTT-CRUZ

My beautiful sweet Adilene
The desires of my heart
The fires of my passion
The hope of my promise
And sacred pledge
To you
My dreams at night
Are only of you
My kisses shared only
With you
My lover and giver
Of life
My sweetest, my dearest
Adilene
My devotions follow
You
My heart is bound
To you
My hope, my trust
Belong to you
My love remains true

Love Infuses Heart And Soul

BY JEFFREY ELLIOTT-CRUZ

Love tis a matter
Of the heart's desire
The hearts fancy adorns
The soul with love's grace
Finer than any richly
Laden cloths
For love is the heart's
Beautifully dressed attire
Truly
Love is the key
To the soul
Like a beautiful celestial
Cord from heaven to earth
Love manifests heavens earth
When true lover's embrace
Heaven is a place
 In the lover's heart
A symbol of God's
Affairs on earth
Love infuses heart and soul

Is The Greatest Of All God's Gifts

BY JEFFREY ELLIOTT-CRUZ

The taste of love
Is always sweet
The souls most purest
Emotion expressed
Love transforms
The most bitter moment
Into monumental behest
For love uplifts
The most depressed spirit
Provides faith and hope
To overcome obstacles
Love is the greatest
Of all God's gifts

LOVE REMAINS

Love's Circle - Epilogue

BY JEFFREY ELLIOTT-CRUZ

Although dearest loved ones
May walk upon this mortal sphere
Or departed to dwell in God's presence

In a more holy exalted home
Loved ones are never forgotten
The family circle attained
But our love always remains
Written upon the tablet
Of our heart in a sanctified
Way
Never to forget
A circle of unending everlasting love
A forever memory and happy place
For love never fades or separates
Love's holy circle
As true love remains

The Beauty

BY JEFFREY ELLIOTT-CRUZ

The soul often reflects
The beauty of the woman
The grace and sweetness
 Of her lovely countenance
 Coupled with the fortitude
 Of her divine spark
 Like healing balm
 For eyes and heart
 Gentleness combined
 With picturesque beauty
 Summons courage
 To enjoy her as celestial
  art
  A masterpiece of God›s
  divine divinity
  An appropation
  Of delicate beauty
  And refined emotions
  and feeling
  A heavenly masterpiece

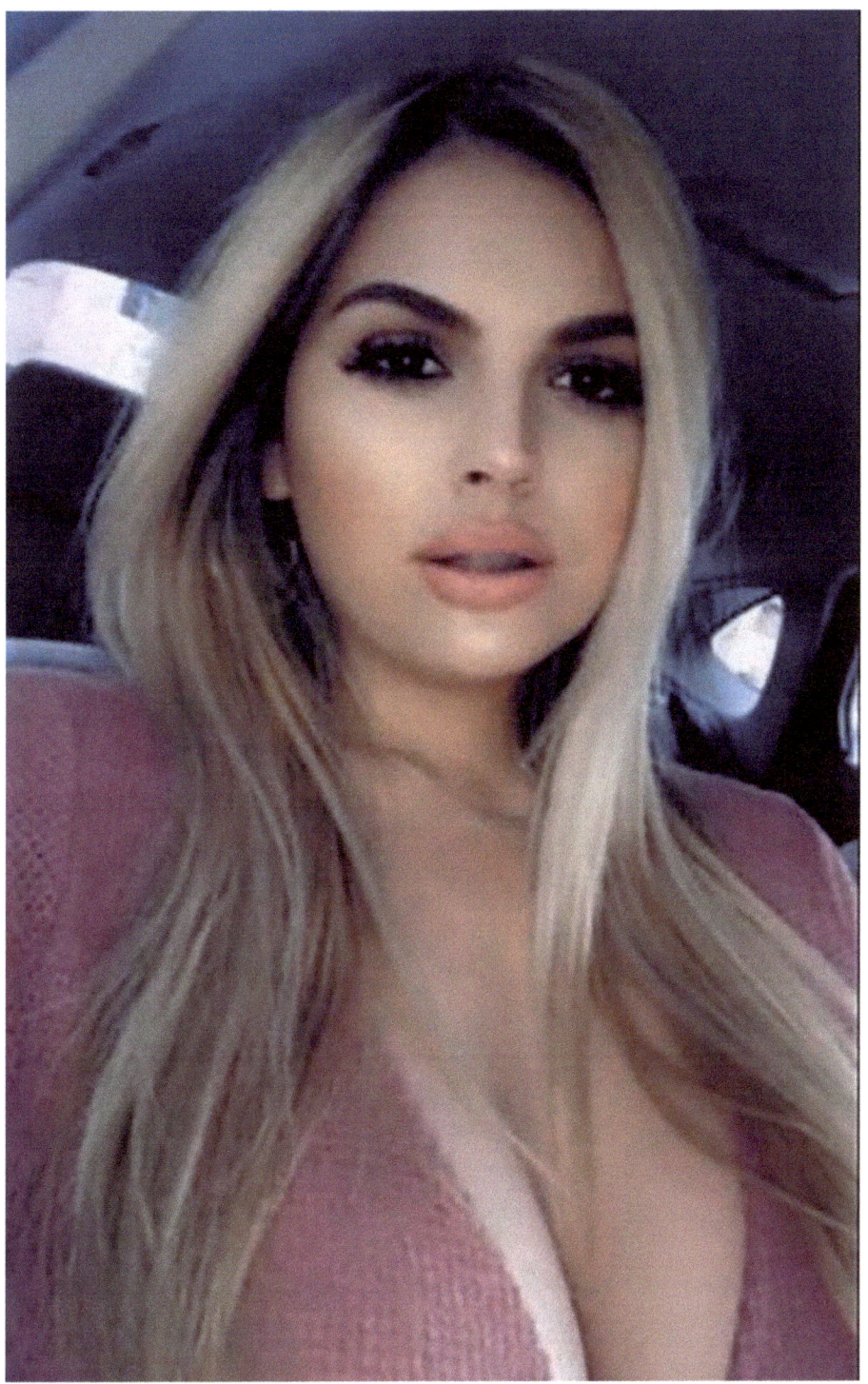

My Heart Belongs To You

BY JEFFREY ELLIOTT-CRUZ

In everytime, in everyway, everyday and with everyone
My heart belongs to you
The rythmn of my heart
Beats in time with your song
My soul is filled with your rhyme
My kisses are for your lips
My ears listen to your desires
My heart is aflame with the music of your soul
My prayers are for you
My soul is yearning
To embrace you
My heart belongs to you

A Time Of Love

BY JEFFREY ELLIOTT-CRUZ

In the spring time
Of life
Beauty shines
Before life's winter fades
Often captured in a glance
Is the beauty
Which never fades
But as love remains

A Pledge

BY JEFFREY ELLIOTT-CRUZ

As the God's favor
Strength from their glory
And mother earth rejoices
In her offspring
Life is sweeter in your
Presence
More happiness satisfaction complete
Our pledge of fealty and loyalty
Will bind our hearts as one
Guide our trust and commitment
Warm as the sun as bright as the God's in their glory
Nurtured by mother earth
For a place and space
To love and be loved
Forever the pledge

My Love Overflows

BY JEFFREY ELLIOTT-CRUZ

My love for you
Is as a stream
Which overflows
Cascading as a waterfall
Waters of love
Cleansing my heart
With purity and virtue
I will lie with no other
My heart is reserved
Especially for you
Like pure waters
Flowing as my love
Towards you increases
In purity and joy
I shall taste of no
Others lips nor kisses
For all my joys are only
With you
My life and love
Belong to your heart
My love Overflows for you

Love Is Always

BY JEFFREY ELLIOTT-CRUZ

A lover's paradise
Lies beyond the material
World
Beyond fate, fame and fortune
A lover's garden of Eden
A paradise of mutual understanding
Respect , loyalty and faithfulness
Love blossoms
As the lovely Rose
In a lover's garden
With lasting peace
In the valley of Sharon
As a lover's paradise
Bound by the bond of love
For love is always
The finest flower
In Eden's garden

Minutes

BY JEFFREY ELLIOTT-CRUZ

My heart counts the minutes
That I am separated from you
My heart yearns in seconds
The time away from you
My soul is anguished
When I am out of your
presence
Time away from you
Is slow and burdensome
When I am in your arms
Enjoy your embrace and
Kisses
Time moves swiftly hours
turn to minutes,
Minutes to seconds
The eternities are insufficient
To enjoy my lover›s touch
And to feel her embrace
Life moves swiftly
Within my lover›s embrace

The Depth Of Love

BY JEFFREY ELLIOTT-CRUZ

Life nor death
Will separate us
Life and breath
May depart from us
But our love everlasting
Shall lay hold of us
Bonds of infinity
Will hold our love
Though death may
 overcome
The depth of God's love
Shall bring our salvation
The bonds of our love
Shall bind us through out
Time
And seal our hearts together
In all eternity
Death shall not separate us
But our love shall empower us
And bind us together
For all time and in eternity
Our hearts shall be sealed together forever
By the power , hope and faith
 of our hearts
Through the depth of love

Close To You

BY JEFFREY ELLIOTT-CRUZ

Let me walk with you
My love
Let me touch your hair
My love
Let us feel the spring air
My love
Let us pause and enjoy
Each flower my love
The sweetly fragranced air
Let me hear the beat
Of your heart , my lover
Taste your luscious lips
My love
Pause, and give thanks
That I am close to you

Eterity In Your Eyes

BY JEFFREY ELLIOTT-CRUZ

Love wonderfully echoes
In my heart
I see eternity in you're eyes
A heavenly bond
Born in love
Bound by promises
Of faithful fidelity
Two hearts intertwined
With one love
For each other
As a mirror reflects
Eternity in our eyes
The echoes of love
Sounds forever

Love In Essence

BY JEFFREY ELLIOTT-CRUZ

Love, like her close sisters
Faith and hope
Love in essence
Is unseen
By the view
From the material eye
Yet powerfully felt
Beautifully moved
Gracefully manifest
Through the things
Of the unseen spirit
And evidenced by action

My Peach
BY JEFFREY ELLIOTT-CRUZ

In a delightful garden
Is a strong tree
Which bares sweet peaches
My lover is the most delicious
Peach on the tree
In the garden
She is the sweetest fruit
In this heavenly garden

My Lover's Gentle Touch
BY JEFFREY ELLIOTT-CRUZ

Love shapes and chisels
The soul like the sculptor's master touch
My lover's touch
Gently refines my soul
As the master sculptor's
loving touch
Shapes his masterpiece
As an artist's work
In God's gentle divine hands
By my lover's gentle touch
My lover shapes my destiny
As her refined masterpiece
According to celestial purpose
In God's divine heavenly plan

Adilene's Faith

BY JEFFREY ELLIOTT-CRUZ

The fiery flame of passion
Influences the destiny
Of God's children
In mortality
To progress forward
In God's heavenly plan
Sometimes life's path
Are strewn with challenges
And obstacles, setbacks, disappointments and heartaches
And the pain of heartbreaks
Death, and breakups, broken dreams, emptiness and suffering
To survive means trusting
God's eternal plan
Adilene's faith and prayer
Has brought her to
That place here
To trust in God's
Eternal plan

LOVE REMAINS

My Heart Can Never Let You Go

BY JEFFREY ELLIOTT-CRUZ

My life and my blood,
My Soul and my spirit,
Belongs with you're heart
Only to you,
I bequeath my heartbeat
I yearn
To be with you,
Eternal lover,
My hearts fondest dreams
My soul's hunger
Is satisfied
 Only by your love
My thirst quenched
Only by your companionship
My soul is greeted
In joy by happiness
In the warmth
Of your everlasting love
God's gift complete
My true lover,
My heart can never
Let you go

Love Means Forgiveness

BY JEFFREY ELLIOTT-CRUZ

Love is a gentle companion
And works with a kindly voice
Empathy and compassion
Enjoyable with an abundance of graciousness
Is slow to anger, mock and ridicule

Love embraces kindness, tenderness and unrelenting patience
Love avoids deceit, ridicule and excessively harsh criticism
Love is merciful and forgiving
Love is embraced by faith and hope
Love means forgiveness

True Lover's Serenade

BY JEFFREY ELLIOTT-CRUZ

In the misty moonlight
My heart yearns for your kiss
I will tell you of my love
For you
And call upon you with respect
To honor you and your family
Never to declare a false promise
To satiate base lust
But rather,
I will call upon you
To honor you and to keep
My promises to you
Not to offend honor and love
By lustful intentions and false promises
A true lover's word
In the Misty moonlight

Love Is A Time Of Innocence

BY JEFFREY ELLIOTT-CRUZ

My love for you
Is within a time of innocent
My desire for your embrace
Is in a time of edification and dedication
To express my hearts
Feelings of true emotion
To seal my kiss
With your exaltation
And bring me your salvation

An eternal dedication
To your solemn devotion
My love flows
In our innovative innocence
The essence of our elevation
To our loving devotion

In God's Light

BY JEFFREY ELLIOTT-CRUZ

Only your purity
Exceeds your beauty
Only your gracious kindness
Exceeds your benevolence
In lover's dedication
I wish you joy and blessings
And bless you with God's
Protection and strength
So that when fierce winds
Threaten your peace and happiness,
To drown you in life's troubles
God will grant you wisdom
To survive, to thrive, to strive
And choose a higher path
A heavenly road full of faith
Manifests your pure heart
You're purity and beauty,
Lovely Adi, daughter of God,
Rose of Sharon ,
Embraced and bathed
In a more holy way
In God's light

Her Love Is My Declaration

BY JEFFREY ELLIOTT-CRUZ

My lover brings
My heart joy
My lover brings
My soul to life,
My lover protects
My spirit and increases
My minds nourishment
My lover helps me understand
My life's dimension
My love for her
Is beyond comprehension
She is my highest valuation
By extreme exaltation
A delight to my sensations
My life's comfort
And excitation
She is my exclamation
Her love is forever my declaration
She is my satisfaction

Healing Rose Of Sharon

BY JEFFREY ELLIOTT-CRUZ

My lover has filled my soul
With sublime joy
True happiness
And the peace
Of eternal companionship
My lovely desert rose
Has removed the suffering,
Painful and hurtful thorns
From my soul and heart
And left her sweet fragrance
Of comfort and compassion
Filled the empty places
Of loneliness and despair
With the sweetness of
Companionship and
A foundation of emotional
Support, trust and loyalty
My lovely healing
Rose of Sharon

Passions Of Desire

BY JEFFREY ELLIOTT-CRUZ

Tis not the first kiss
That ignites the passions
Tis not the first physical touch
That lights the embers of desire
It is the true conversations,
Between lovers
For lovers begin their journey
In a conversation of the hearts
Which satisfies souls and minds
And mingles hearts together
Into a spiritual union of lovers
Through quiet deeds of kindness
And feelings of empathy
To care and forge a path together
Which truly enflames
Hearts and passions of desire

Silent Moments

BY JEFFREY ELLIOTT-CRUZ

In the silent moments
When thoughts are stilled
And feelings are muted
Love songs play
In the hearts symphony hall
To the soul's audience
Which move the mind's ear
To stir the heart,
To tears of enjoyment and emotion
Sorrow and surrender
Longing and desire
During those silent moments

www.ingramcontent.com/pod-product-compliance
Lightning Source LLC
LaVergne TN
LVHW051225070526
838200LV00057B/4609